Speak in a Week™
Spanish
Week One

Designed by Donald S. Rivera
Illustrated by Julie Bradbury

Produced & distributed by

Penton Overseas, Inc.
Carlsbad, CA

Speak in a Week®
Spanish:
Week One

Published and distributed by Penton Overseas, Inc.,
1958 Kellogg Ave., Carlsbad, CA 92008.
www.pentonoverseas.com

Contact publisher by phone at (800) 748-5804
or via email, info@pentonoverseas.com.

ISBN 1-59125-285-7

Lessons:

How to Use Speak in a Week:

Start with **Lesson One.** If you've studied Spanish before, you'll move on more quickly. Follow the lessons in order so you learn everything well. Master each lesson before you go to the next one.

Each lesson begins with an outline of what you'll be learning, followed by ten illustrated examples, first in Spanish, then in English. For every lesson, there's a track on the audio–CD to help you with Spanish pronunciation.

On the illustrated pages, you'll also find extra grammar tips, helpful hints, and interesting facts about Spanish-speaking cultures. Following the eight lessons, you'll find a reference section with basic info, more words, and extra grammar.

When you've finished the lessons, go to the audio CD and listen to the last five tracks: **The Mastery Exercises.** You'll play with the Spanish you now know, so that you'll be able to make new sentences from what you've learned.

You'll be speaking Spanish!

Lesson 1

In this lesson you will learn...

- basic greetings
  - ☞ **Hola, Buenos días, Buenas tardes, etc.**

- to meet someone and make introductions
  - ☞ **¿Cómo se llama?, Me llamo..., etc.**

- different ways to say good-bye
  - ☞ **Adiós, Hasta luego, Hasta mañana, etc.**

Tips For Using Speak in a Week!

• Master one lesson at a time. Make sure you are comfortable with all of the vocabulary and grammatical concepts in each lesson before moving on to the next.

• Expand your vocabulary! Add the Glossary Section into your study program when instructed to do so.

• Practice each lesson out loud. Use the phonetic guides and audio CD to help you practice speaking.

• If you have the opportunity, practice with a partner.

Most of all, take your time and make learning Spanish fun.

¡Buenos días!
bweh-nohs dee-ahs

The key to sounding good in Spanish is in the vowels. Try to pronounce them short and crisp, without using a lot of air.

Good Morning!

Pages 179-80 will teach you the different Sounds of Spanish. Use them as an easy reference guide for pronunciation.

In Spanish, an inverted question mark (¿) precedes a question. An inverted exclamation mark (¡) precedes an exclamation.

Good afternoon!

Your pronunciation may not be perfect at first. That's okay! Practice with the CD and repeat the words OUT LOUD!

¡Buenas noches!
bweh-nahs noh-chehs

¡Buenas noches! is used
as both a greeting,
Good evening!
and to bid farewell,
Good night!

7

Listen carefully to how native Spanish speakers greet each other. You'll pick up many new greetings in a hurry!

Usted (you) is a formal form of speech, used with someone you don't know very well or as a sign of respect

11

In Spanish, you may address another person using either a formal or informal form of speech.

12

Tú (you) is an informal form of speech, used with friends, family, and others with whom you are on a first-name basis.

13

Throughout this program, *informal*, written below or after the word *you*, indicates use of the informal form of address.

14

Another way to say What is your name? is: ¿Cuál es su nombre? Respond with: Mi nombre es... (My name is...).

Many Spanish speakers have two family names: their father's family name, followed by their mother's maiden name.

16

¡Mucho gusto!
moo-choh goo-stoh

¡Igualmente!
ee-gwahl-mehn-teh

Try saying the Spanish words without using the phonetic guide. Then, refer to the guide and see how close you came.

17

Spanish speakers generally shake hands when greeting each other and also when saying goodbye.

18

"Adiós" literally means "to God", and is generally used when you do not plan on seeing the person for a while.

19

There are many ways to greet someone in Spanish. For a list of frequently used Greetings and Courtesies, see page 233.

20

Careful! Mañana means both tomorrow and in the morning. To say, tomorrow in the morning say: mañana en la mañana.

21

To benefit the most from this program, be sure
to master each lesson before beginning the next!

Lesson 2

In this lesson you will learn...

- basic survival phrases
- ☞ **Sí, No, ¿Entiende?, No entiendo, ¿Cómo se dice...?, etc.**

- common expressions of courtesy
- ☞ **Gracias, De nada, Por favor, Con permiso, etc.**

Tips For Learning SPANISH!

- **Practice Often** – Your effort is the most important factor in this program. Make a daily appointment to study and keep it!

- **Immerse Yourself** – Learn as much as you can about the culture and its people. Tune in to Spanish television and radio and practice with audio CDs.

- **Find a Spanish-Speaking Friend** – Most Spanish-speakers enjoy helping learners of Spanish and feel good that you are trying to speak their language. Thus, they are often very willing to help you practice, errors and all!

- **Be Patient** – Learning to speak Spanish may seem a little difficult at first, but rest assured, it will become less and less "foreign" with a little time and a lot of practice.

Notice that Sí has an accent over the í.
Si without an accent means if.

25

Spanish speakers may use body language such as moving their pointer finger back and forth to emphasize, "No!"

The Spanish **v** is a cross between **v** and **b**. It is pronounced with the lips slightly parted, much like the **v** in mauve.

27

Be courteous at all times and don't forget to say please.
Courtesy and respect will take you far in any language.

Literally translated, de nada means for nothing. You may also say por nada, which means the same thing.

Don't be surprised if your Spanish friend uses a different word. Vocabulary varies greatly by country and region.

Use perdóname if you bump into someone. But if you want to squeeze past someone, say: con permiso (excuse me).

31

Pardon me!

Don't be intimidated by pronunciation. Try for your best accent and start speaking. You'll sound better each time.

At first you might find yourself asking,
¿Habla inglés? (Do you speak English?)

Did you know? There are 21 Spanish-speaking countries, and more than 300 million people who speak Spanish!

Just fill in the blank with the word you want to know and you'll be able to ask for any word you need.

Don't be afraid to ask a lot of questions and then let the words fly! You'll learn much faster and have a lot more fun.

¿Cómo se deletrea?
koh-moh seh deh-leh-**treh**-ah

Ask them to spell it, letra por letra (letter by letter). For a quick review of the Spanish Alphabet, see page 177.

How do you spell it?

Did you know? Spanish, along with French, Italian and other Romance languages, all stem from vulgar (spoken) Latin.

¿Cúal es el número de teléfono?
*kwahl ehs ehl **noo**-meh-roh deh teh-**leh**-foh-noh*

If you're having a difficult time understanding a number, ask for it one number at a time – número por número, por favor.

What is the telephone number?

555-1212

Make sure you include the Numbers (pages 185-90) in your words to learn this week. They're a must for survival.

¡Repita por favor!

*reh-**pee**-tah pohr fah-**vohr***

You can also say, más despacio (more slowly), or, if you just didn't hear what was said, ask: ¿Cómo? or ¿Qué? (What?)

At first, Spanish may sound like the words all run together. Don't worry – you'll be running yours together in no time!

If you understand the question being asked, but don't know the answer, just say: ¡No sé! (I don't know.).

43

Be sure to master the greetings and survival phrases in the first two lessons before beginning the next.

Lesson 3

In this lesson you will learn...

- to ask where something or someone is located
  ☞ **¿Dónde está…?**

- to talk about likes and dislikes (singular)
  ☞ **Me gusta, ¿Le gusta?, No me gusta**

- about gender and the two singular articles for the word the
  ☞ **masculine/feminine, el and la**

In Spanish, all nouns are classified by gender as either masculine or feminine. (See **page 183** for an explanation of **Gender**.) The article *the* for singular nouns is expressed as either *el* or *la* depending on the gender of the noun to which it refers.

Masculine Nouns

el niño (the boy)
el libro (the book)
el hotel (the hotel)
el color (the color)

Feminine Nouns

la niña (the girl)
la pluma (the pen)
la ciudad (the city)
la lección (the lesson)

Be sure to look over **page 183**
before starting this lesson.

¿Dónde está... ?

dohn-deh eh-stah

el teléfono?
*ehl teh-**leh**-foh-noh*

el baño?
*ehl **bah**-nyoh*

As a general rule, use **el** to express *the* for singular nouns ending with the letter –o

Where is... ?

the **telephone**

the **bathroom**

Master a couple of Glossary pages with each lesson and by the end of this program, you'll be able to talk about almost anything.

48

¿Dónde está... ?
dohn-deh eh-stah

la mesa
lah meh-sah

la silla
lah see-yah

As a general rule, use **la** to express **the** for singular nouns ending in –a.

Where is... ?

the table

the chair

Practice the vocabulary words on pages 211-12 by making signs and labeling all of the Furniture in your home.

¿Dónde está... ?

dohn-deh eh-stah

el niño

*ehl **nee**-nyoh*

la niña

*ehl **nee**-nyah*

Use el to express the for singular nouns referring to males and la for singular nouns referring to females.

51

Where is... ?

the **boy**

the **girl**

If you are referring to an older boy or girl say:
el muchacho or la muchacha.

52

¿Dónde está... ?
dohn-deh eh-stah

el señor García
ehl seh-nyohr gahr-see-ah

la señora García?
ehl seh-nyohr-rah gahr-see-ah

The articles **el** and **la** accompany a title except when addressing the person directly. (¡Buenos días señor García!)

Where is... ?

Mr. García

Mrs. García

The Spanish word for Miss is señorita, and refers to an unmarried woman. There is no word for Ms, yet!

¿Dónde está... ?
dohn-deh eh-stah

la clase
lah klah-seh

el restaurante
ehl reh-stow-rahn-teh

It's best to learn the article (el, la) right along with the noun, especially for words not ending in –o or –a.

Where is... ?

the class

the restaurant

You'll be surprised at how many Spanish words you already know or can easily recognize.

¿Le gusta... ?
leh goo-stah

la música?
lah moo-see-kah

la fiesta?
lah fyeh-sta

The accent mark over the **ú** in música means to say that part of the word louder.

Do you like... ?

the music

the party

Did you know? The popular disco music of the 70s originated from the Latin rhythms of Cuba and the Caribbean.

Me gusta...

*meh **goo**-stah*

la sopa

*lah **soh**-pah*

la ensalada

*lah ehn-sah-**lah**-dah*

Definite articles (el, la) are used even when referring to something in general: Me gusta la sopa. (I like soup.).

I like...

the **soup**

the **salad**

While eating, this sentence refers to the soup or salad being eaten. If said when not eating, it refers to soup or salad in general.

¿Le gusta... ?
*leh **goo**-stah*

el libro?
*ehl **lee**-broh*

el museo?
*ehl moo-**seh**-oh*

To ask friend if he or she likes something say: ¿Te gusta...?
You'll learn more about le and te when you get to Lesson 29.

61

Do you like... ?

the **book**

the **museum**

Use this lesson to tune your "ear" to gender by saying each word (with its article) over and over again.

Me gusta...
*meh **goo**-stah*

el parque
*ehl **pahr**-keh*

la playa
*lah **plah**-yah*

The letter combination **qu** is always pronouced like the **k** in **kite**.

I like...

the **park**

the **beach**

Before you leave to the park or the beach, you may want to check out The Weather on pages 193-94

No me gusta...
*noh meh **goo**-stah*

el hotel
*ehl oh-**tehl***

el café
*ehl kah-**feh***

Use the articles **el** and **la** even when referring to something in general: No me gusta el café. (I don't like coffee.)

I don't like...

the **hotel**

coffee

Make sure you're comfortable with vocabulary and
grammatical principles presented in this lesson before
moving on to the next.

Lesson 4

In this lesson you will learn...

- to ask where people and things are located

  ☞ ¿Dónde están...?

- to talk about likes and dislikes (plural)

  ☞ Me gustan, ¿Le gustan?, etc...

- to use the two plural articles for the word *the*

  ☞ los, las

In Spanish, the article *the* for plural nouns can be expressed as either *los* or *las*. Use *los* to refer to *masculine* nouns and *las* to refer to *feminine* nouns. (See **page 183**.)

Masculine Nouns		Feminine Nouns	
Singular	**Plural**	**Singular**	**Plural**
el niño	*los* niños	*la* niña	*las* niñas
el libro	*los* libros	*la* pluma	*las* plumas
el hotel	*los* hoteles	*la* ciudad	*las* ciudades
el color	*los* colores	*la* lección	*las* lecciones

Note: a noun is made plural by adding **–s** if it ends in a vowel, and **–es** if it ends in a consonant. (*See above.*)

¿Dónde están... ?

dohn-deh eh-stahn

los niños

*lohs **nee**-nyohs*

las niñas

*lahs **nee**-nyahs*

Use el or la for singular nouns only! For plural nouns, use los and las (el niño – los niños / la niña – las niñas).

Where are... ?

the **boys**

the **girls**

If you are referring to older boys or girls say:
los muchachos or las muchachas.

72

¿Dónde están... ?

dohn-deh eh-stahn

los **hombres**
*lohs **ohm**-brehs*

las **mujeres**
*lahs moo-**heh**-rehs*

Use los to express plural nouns referring to males and las for plural nouns referring to females.

Where are... ?

the men

the women

To refer to ladies say: las señoras or las damas.
To refer to gentlemen say: los caballeros.

¿Dónde están... ?

dohn-deh eh-stahn

los **boletos**
*lohs bo-**leh**-tohs*

los **regalos**
*lohs reh-**gah**-lohs*

Train you ear, and the articles become easy. Just remember los (lohs) goes with words ending with the sound ohs.

Where are... ?

the **tickets**

the **gifts**

Another word for tickets is las entradas. If you are specifically referring to tickets for a train or an airplane say: los billetes.

¿Dónde están... ?

dohn-deh eh-stahn

las **revistas**
*lahs reh-**vee**-stahs*

las **tiendas**
lahs tyehn-dohs

Just listen to the rhyme and remember that las (lahs)
goes with words ending with the sound ahs.

Where are... ?

the **magazines**

the **stores**

Stop by one of The Stores on pages 231-32 and pick up the Everyday Necessities you'll need on pages 201-02.

¿Dónde están... ?

dohn-deh eh-stahn

los pasajeros
lohs pah-sah-heh-rohs

las maletas
lahs mah-leh-tahs

Practice saying the words out loud and notice how the articles just sound right. (**Lohs** with **ohs** and **lahs** with **ahs**.)

Where are... ?

the **passengers**

the **suitcases**

Sometimes you just have to get away. Get ready for all your Trips & Travel with pages 215-16.

¿Dónde están... ?
dohn-deh eh-stahn

las llaves
lahs yah-behs

los paquetes
lohs pah-keh-tehs

Many nouns do not follow the guidelines for gender. It's best to learn the matching article (el, la, los, las) as you learn the noun.

Where are...?

the **keys**

the **packages**

Want to send a little gift home? Well, first you need to locate your keys...then hurry to The Post Office on pages 220-21.

¿Le gustan... ?

leh goo-stahn

las **fresas**
*lahs **freh**-sahs*

las **galletas**
*lahs gah-**yeh**-tahs*

You must use a definite article (el, la, los, las) before the noun even when referring to something in general.

Do you like... ?

strawberries

cookies

Pick any of the Fruit you like on pages 207-08. But if you really want to splurge, head for the Desserts on page 206.

Me gustan...

meh goo-stahn

las montañas
*lahs mohn-**tah**-nyahs*

los árboles
*lohs **ahr**-boh-lehs*

To form the plural, add –s to nouns ending in a vowel and –es to nouns ending in a consonant.

I like...

the **mountains**

the **trees**

The concept of masculine and feminine is used for classification only and has no relation to an object's physical characteristics.

¿Le gustan... ?
leh goo-stahn

las flores
lahs floh-rehs

las rosas
lahs roh-sahs

Remember: You must use a definite article (el, la, los, las) before a noun even when referring to something in general.

Do you like... ?

flowers

roses

Build your vocabulary quickly by substituting words from the Glossary for the words you learned in this lesson!

No me gustan...
noh meh goo-stahn

los perros
lohs peh-rrohs

los gatos
lohs gah-tohs

When referring to plural nouns, ¿Le gusta...?
changes to ¿Le gustan...? and ¿Dónde está...?
changes to ¿Dónde están...?

I don't like...

dogs

cats

Remember: Carry the book with you and study until you can express plurals with ease. Then move on to Lesson 5.

Lesson 5

In this lesson you will learn...

- to talk about things you *need*, *want*, and *have* ☞ **Necesito, Quiero, Tengo**

- to express the concept of *a* ☞ **un, una**

- to express the concept of *some* ☞ **unos, unas**

In Spanish, the indefinite articles *un*, *una* (a) and *unos*, *unas* (some) must agree in gender and number with the nouns to which they refer. Use *un* and *unos* to refer to masculine nouns and *una* and *unas* to refer to feminine nouns.

Masculine Nouns

un niño *(a boy)*
unos niños *(**some** boys)*
un libro *(a book)*
unos libros *(**some** books)*

Feminine Nouns

una niña *(**a** girl)*
unas niñas *(**some** girls)*
una pluma *(**a** pen)*
unas plumas *(**some** pens)*

For a review on determining the **Gender** of a noun,
see **page 183**.

Necesito...

*neh-seh-**see**-toh*

un vaso
*oon **vah**-soh*

un plato
*oon **plah**-toh*

To express "a" for singular masculine nouns, say **un**. Remember: The letter **v** sounds like a cross between a **b** and a **v**.

I need...

a glass

a plate

Having guests for dinner? For additional items you might need to Set The Table see pages 213-14.

Necesito...

neh-seh-see-toh

una pluma

oo-nah ploo-mah

una toalla

oo-nah twah-yah

To express "a" for singular feminine nouns, say **una**.
In Spanish the double letters **ll** sound like a **y**, as in **yet**.

I need...

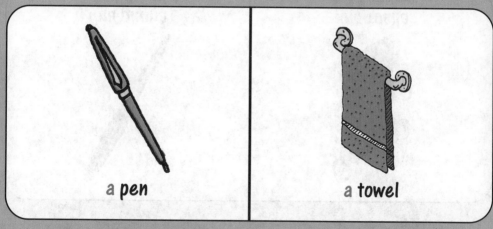

a pen

a towel

Another word for a pen is un bolígrafo.

Necesito...
neh-seh-see-toh

unos zapatos
oo-nohs sah-pah-tohs

unas botas
oo-nahs boh-tahs

The plural form of un is unos (some).
The plural form of una is unas (some).

I need...

some **shoes**

some **boots**

Need some new socks? How about a new belt?
Check out the Clothing and Jewelry on pages 197-200.

Necesito...

*neh-seh-**see**-toh*

un menú

*oon **meh**-noo*

un lápiz

*oon **lah**-pees*

Learn the article with the noun, almost as if they were one word. This is especially important for nouns not ending in –o or –a.

I need...

a menu

a pencil

Study Tip: Writing these phrases over and over in Spanish will help cement them in you memory.

Quiero...
kyeh-roh

una cerveza
*oo-nah sehr-**veh**-sah*

una bebida
*oo-nah beh-**bee**-dah*

Use Yo (I) to clarify or to emphasize the subject of a sentence. Yo quiero una cerveza. (I want a beer.)

I want...

a beer

a drink

Okay! Time to take a short break. Order up a drink from the Beverages on pages 204-05 and just relax!

Quiero...
kyeh-roh

un sandwich
oon san-weech

un helado
oon eh-lah-doh

Sandwich is commonly understood in many countries. It may also be called una torta (Mexico) and un bocadillo (Spain).

I want

a sandwich

an ice cream

The pronunciation guides disappear after Lesson 8, so pay attention to how the Spanish letters are pronounced.

Quiero...
kyeh-roh

unas manzanas
oo-nahs mahn-sah-nahs

unos plátanos
oo-nohs plah-tah-nohs

The word for banana in Spain is plátano. In some countries, however, plátano is used to refer to a large cooking banana.

I want...

some **apples**

some **bananas**

Whether it's a pound or a handful, you can get exactly the Portions & Measurements you need with page 230.

Tengo...
tehn-goh

un hijo
oon ee-hoh

una hija
oo-nah ee-hah

Watch your pronunciation! The letter **j** sounds like the **h** in **hat** and the letter **h** is silent.

I have...

a **son**

a **daughter**

Talking about family is a great icebreaker. See pages 195-96 for a list of other Family Members you might want to brag about.

Tengo...
tehn-goh

un problema
oon proh-bleh-mah

una pregunta
oo-nah preh-goon-tah

Problema is an exception to the gender rules. Make sure you say, el problema, un problema, and unos problemas.

I have...

a problem

a question

Be patient! In Lesson 12 you'll learn
how to ask all the questions you want.

No tengo...

noh tehn-goh

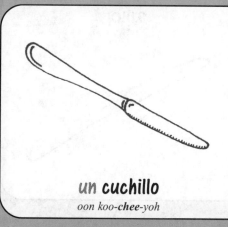

un cuchillo

oon koo-chee-yoh

una servilleta

oo-nah sehr-vee-yeh-tah

Now try to combine concepts from one lesson with others.
Mastery Exercise: No tengo las llaves.

I don't have...

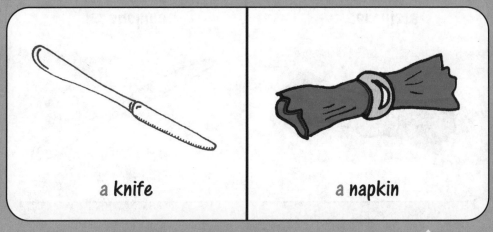

a knife

a napkin

Mastery Exercise: I don't have the keys. You'll find more
chances to test your mastery in the pages ahead.

Lesson 6

In this lesson you will learn...

- to talk about what other people *have*, *want* and *need*
  - ☞ ¿Tiene?, ¿Quiere?, ¿Necesita?

- to indicate to whom something belongs: *my*, *your*, *his*, *her*, *their*, *its*, *Alicia's*, etc.
  - ☞ mi, mis, su, sus, "de" Alicia, etc.

In Spanish, the possessive adjectives *mi*, *mis* (*my*) and *su*, *sus* (*his, her, your, their, and its*) must agree in **number** with the noun to which they refer.

Singular	**Plural**
mi libro (*my* book)	*mis* libros (*my* books)
su libro (*your* book)	*sus* libros (*your* books)
su libro (*his* book)	*sus* libros (*his* books)
su libro (*her* book)	*sus* libros (*her* books)
su libro (*their* book)	*sus* libros (*their* books)

To express possession in Spanish, (*Maria's book*), the preposition *de* (*of*) is used in front of the noun and the word order is reversed.

(El libro de María – The book of Maria)

¿Tiene... ?

tyeh-neh

mi maleta

mee mah-leh-tah

mis boletos

mees boh-leh-tohs

The word **my** can be expressed as **mi** or **mis**. Use **mi** with singular nouns and **mis** with plural nouns.

Do you have... ?

my **suitcase**

my **tickets**

If you've been mastering previous lessons, suitcase and tickets should already be a part of your Spanish vocabulary.

¿Tiene... ?
tyeh-neh

su billetera
*soo bee-yah-**teh**-rah*

sus llaves
*soos **yah**-vehs*

The word your can be expressed as su or sus. Use
su with singular nouns and sus with plural nouns.

Do you have... ?

your **wallet**

your **keys**

Words for the Everyday Necessities are a must for
your new vocabulary. Learn them with pages 201-02.

¿Tiene... ?

tyeh-neh

su cámara
*soo **kah**-mah-rah*

sus fotos
*soos **foh**-tohs*

The words su and sus can also be used to express her.
(her shoe – su zapato / her shoes – sus zapatos)

Do you have... ?

his **camera**

his **photos**

¿Tiene... ?

tyeh-neh

su dinero
soo dee-neh-roh

sus paquetes
soos pah-keh-tehs

Just think of su and sus as the multi-purpose words of Spanish. They can be used to express his, her, your, their and its.

Do you have... ?

their **money**

their **packages**

Carry the book with you and try to use the words during the day. You'll learn twice as fast!

¿Necesita... ?

*neh-seh-**see**-tah*

su medicina

*soo meh-dee-**see**-nah*

sus pastillas

*soos pah-**stee**-yahs*

Mastery Exercise: ¿Dónde está mi medicina?

Do you need... ?

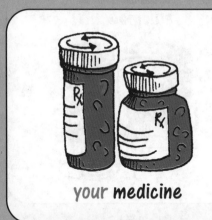

your **medicine**

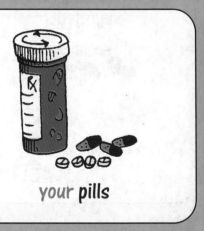

your **pills**

¿Necesita... ?

*neh-seh-**see**-tah*

mi sombrero

*mee sohm-**breh**-roh*

mis anteojos de sol

*mees ahn-teh-**oh**-hohs deh sohl*

If you just want to say *my glasses*, say: mis anteojos.
Another common way of saying *glasses* is los lentes.

Do you need... ?

my **hat**

my **sunglasses**

Be aware! Different Spanish-speaking countries or regions
have variations in vocabulary and pronunciation.

¿Necesita... ?
neh-seh-see-tah

su dirección
soo dee-rehk-syohn

su número de teléfono

It can usually be determined by the context of the conversation whether **su** is being used to mean his, her, your, their, or its.

Do you need... ?

his **address**

their **phone number**

Wondering how to say, our telephone number or our address? You'll learn how to express our in Lesson 7.

¿Quiere... ?
kyeh-reh

su suéter
soo sweh-tehr

sus guantes
soos gwahn-tehs

To be more specific, use de (of) with él (he) or ella (she). el suéter de él (his sweater) – los guantes de ella (her gloves)

Do you want... ?

his sweater
*soo **sweh**-tehr*

her gloves
*soos **gwahn**-tehs*

What talla (size) is your sweater?
Chico, mediano, grande or extra?

¿Quiere... ?

kyeh-reh

su comida

*soo koh-**mee**-dah*

su mesa

*soo **meh**-sah*

For clarity, use de (of) with usted (you) or ellos/ellas (they).
la comida de usted (your food) – la mesa de ellos (their table)

Do you want... ?

your **food**

their **table**

Tell the waiter exactly how you like your food cooked with
Food Preparation and Flavors on page 210.

¿Quiere... ?

kyeh-reh

la chaqueta de Alicia

*lah chah-**keh**-tah de ah-**lee**-see-ah*

If something belongs to someone else, use **de** (of) followed by the name of the person to whom it belongs.

Do you want... ?

Alicia's jacket

In English, we use -'s to show possession (Alicia's jacket).
In Spanish, there are no apostrophes.

Lesson 7

In this lesson you will learn...

- to express the concept of *our*

☞ **nuestro, nuestros nuestra, nuestras**

- to use words of description like *big*, *small*, *black*, *white*, *clean*, *dirty*, etc.

☞ **grande, grandes, pequeño(s), pequeña(s), negro(s), negra(s), blanco(s), blanca(s), etc.**

In Spanish, the possessive adjective *our* changes to agree with the noun it modifies in both *number* and *gender.*

Masculine	*Feminine*
nuestro niño (our boy)	*nuestra niña (our girl)*
nuestros niños (our boys)	*nuestras niñas (our girls)*

Most descriptive adjectives **ending** with the letter **–o** or **–a** change their ending to agree in both **number** and **gender.**

Masculine	*Feminine*
el libro negro (black book)	*la pluma negra (black pen)*
los libros negros (black books)	*las plumas negras (black pens)*

Most Adjectives not **ending** with the letter **–o** or **–a** change to agree only in **number.**

Singular	*Plural*
la casa grande (big house)	*las casas grandes (big houses)*

Adjectives of *quantity* or *number precede* the nouns they describe.
Adjectives of *quality* generally *follow* the nouns they describe.

¿Necesita... ?

neh-seh-see-tah

nuestro carro
nweh-stroh kah-rroh

nuestros pasaportes
nweh-strohs pah-sah-pohr-tehs

Use **nuestro** to refer to masculine singular nouns and **nuestros** to refer to masculine plural nouns.

Do you need... ?

our car

our passports

See the back of the Lesson 7 introduction for a
brief summary of how to use the possessive
adjective our and descriptive adjectives.

¿Tiene...?
tyeh-neh

nuestra habitación?
nweh-strah ah-bee-tah-syohn

nuestras reservaciones?
nweh-strahs reh-sehr-bah-syoh-nehs

Use nuestra to refer to feminine singular nouns
and nuestras to refer to feminine plural nouns.

Do you have... ?

our **room**

our **reservations**

Most English words ending in –tion become Spanish words simply by changing –tion to –ción. Don't forget the accent!

Tengo...
tehn-goh

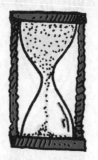

mucho tiempo
moo-choh tyehm-poh

muchos amigos
moo-chohs ah-mee-gohs

Most descriptive adjectives change to match the number of the nouns they describe.

I have...

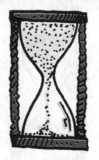

a lot **of** time

a lot **of** friends

In Spanish-speaking countries, it is usually acceptable to arrive at social events well after the appointed time.

¿Quiere... ?

kyeh-reh

otro helado

oh-troh eh-lah-doh

otra bebida

oh-trah beh-bee-dah

Descriptive adjectives ending with the letter –o or –a change to match both the **number** and the **gender** of the noun they describe.

Do you want... ?

another **ice cream**

another **drink**

Learn the Words to Describe on pages 224-29, and you'll be able to describe just about anything or anyone.

142

Quiero...
kyeh-roh

una cerveza grande
*oo-nah **sehr-veh**-sah **grahn**-deh*

dos vasos grandes
*dohs **vah**-sohs **grahn**-deh*

Adjectives of quantity, ie. dos, usually precede the noun.
Adjectives of quality, ie. grande, usually follow the noun.

I want...

a large beer

two large glasses

As you and your amigo clink glasses, say: ¡Salud!

Necesito...
*neh-seh-**see**-toh*

un mapa diferente
*oon **mah**-pah dee-feh-**rehn**-teh*

tres boletos diferentes
*trehs boh-**leh**-tohs dee-feh-**rehn**-tehs*

Most descriptive adjectives ending in –e change only to match the **number** of the noun they describe.

I need...

a **different** map

three **different** tickets

Many English words ending in –ent or –ant become Spanish words simply by adding an –e at the end: -ente, -ante.

146

Tengo...
tehn-goh

pelo negro
peh-loh neh-groh

pantalones negros
pahn-tah-loh-nehs neh-grohs

Colors are adjectives too, and must agree in number and gender with the nouns they describe.

I have...

black **hair**

black **pants**

But what if you have brown hair and green pants? You'll need to know all of the Colors on page 203.

Me gusta...
meh-goo-stah

su blusa blanca
soo bloo-seh blahn-kah

su vestido blanco
soo veh-stee-doh blahn-koh

Remember: The gender of an item has nothing to do with its physical characteristics. **Vestido** is masculine. (It's **el vestido**.)

149

I like...

your white blouse

your white dress

Learning Tip: You can't learn to speak Spanish without speaking it! Be sure to practice saying the words out loud.

¿Necesita... ?
neh-seh-see-tah

un plato limpio
oon plah-toh leem-pyoh

una toalla limpia
oo-nah twah-yah leem-pyah

Don't forget! Descriptive adjectives agree in number and gender. Necesito unas toallas limpias. (I need some clean towels.)

Do you need... ?

a clean plate

a clean towel

If a fork is un tenedor and a spoon is una cuchara, how would you ask for a clean fork or a clean spoon?

Tengo...
tehn-goh

una maleta pequeña
oo-nah mah-leh-tah peh-keh-nyah

un paquete pequeño
oon pah-keh-teh peh-keh-nyoh

Mastery Exercise: Tengo dos perros pequeños.
Remember! The ñ sounds like the ny in canyon.

153

I have...

a small suitcase

a small package

Mastery Exercise: I have two small dogs.

Lesson 8

In this lesson you will...

- Continue to practice expressing the concepts *to have*, *to want*, and *to need*

☞ **Tengo, ¿Tiene?, Quiero, ¿Quiere?, Necesito, ¿Necesita?**

- Learn to connect ideas using the words *and*, *or*, *but*, *with*, *without*, *of*, *in*, *to*, and *for*

☞ **y, o, pero, con, sin, de, en, a, por, para**

Mastery Exercises

After you have mastered this lesson, take some time to review the previous seven lessons. Once you feel comfortable with the vocabulary and grammatical concepts covered in each of the eight lessons, it's time to begin using the Mastery Exercises.

The Mastery Exercises are designed to reinforce what you already know by mixing and matching different language concepts from all eight lessons. Use it to practice and test yourself until you feel confident with all the concepts presented in this first week of Spanish.

Tengo...

tehn-goh

una esposa
oo-nah ehs-poh-sah

y
ee

dos hijos
dohs ee-hohs

The masculine form hijos is used when referring to a mixed group of children. If the children are all girls, use hijas.

157

I have...

a wife **and** two children

In the Hispanic culture, the family unit usually extends to include godparents, in-laws, and even close friends.

¿Quiere... ?
kyeh-reh

la sopa
lah soh-pah

o
oh

la ensalada
lah ehn-sah-lah-dah

In Spanish, words of two or more syllables have only one phonetic stress. Be sure to say that part of the word louder!

Do you want... ?

soup   or   salad

Hungry for something different?
Check out the Main Dishes on page 209.

Tengo...
tehn-goh

No tengo...
no tehn-goh

pero
peh-roh

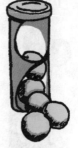

una raqueta
oo-nah rah-keh-tah

una pelota
oo-nah peh-loh-tah

Watch out! Perro (with rr) means dog,

I have...   I don't have...

a racket

but

a ball

With Sports and Equipment, pages 222-23, you can talk about your favorite sport and get all the right equipment.

¿Tiene... ?
tyeh-neh

con
kohn

una habitación
oo-nah ah-bee-tah-syohn

una vista
oo-nah vee-stah

Con connects with mi, ti and si to form conmigo
(with me), contigo (with you – familiar) and consigo
(with you, him, her, them).

Do you have... ?

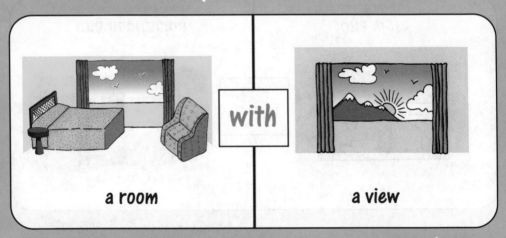

| a room | with | a view |

Learn each part of the example separately. You will soon discover one language concept can be substituted for another.

164

Quiero...
kyeh-roh

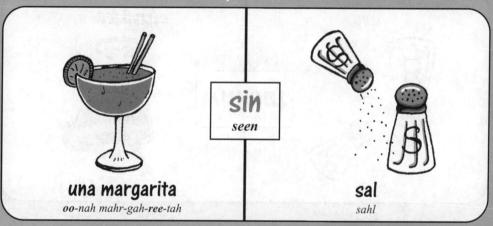

sin
seen

una margarita
oo-nah mahr-gah-ree-tah

sal
sahl

Remember: the opposite of sin is con (with).
Quiero una margarita con sal. (I want a margarita with salt.)

I want...

a margarita — without — salt

Margarita is not only the name of a popular drink, it can also mean the name Margaret, or the flower daisy.

¿Necesita... ?

*neh-seh-**see**-tah*

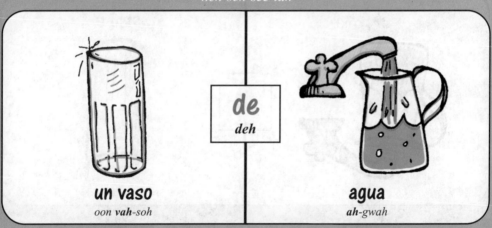

	de	
un vaso	*deh*	**agua**
*oon **vah**-soh*		***ah**-gwah*

Mastery Exercise: ¿Necesita otro vaso de agua?

Do you need... ?

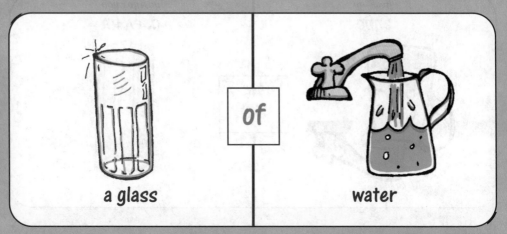

a glass | of | water

Mastery Exercise: Do you need another glass of water?

Tengo...
tehn-goh

en
ehn

una mapa
oo-nah mah-pah

mi mochila
mee moh-chee-lah

The Spanish word en can also mean at, on, or upon.

I have...

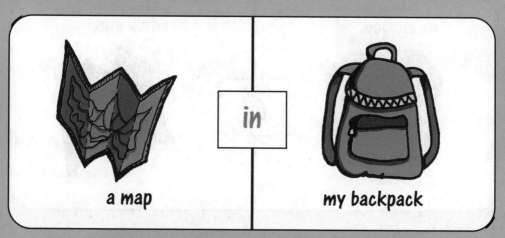

	in	
a map		my backpack

Pack your backpack and your map and explore the things you'll find In the Country on page 217.

¿Dónde está...?

dohn-deh ehs-tah

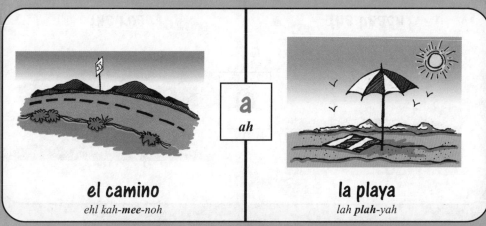

a
ah

el camino
ehl kah-mee-noh

la playa
lah plah-yah

When **a** (to) is used before the article **el** (the), they form the contraction **al** (to the) as in "al hotel" (to the hotel).

Where is... ?

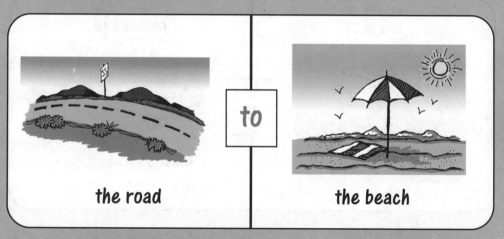

the road | to | the beach

If you plan on travelling in a Spanish-speaking country, you'll need to know the Travel & Road Signs on pages 218-219.

Necesito...

neh-seh-see-toh

una mesa
oo-nah meh-sah

para
pah-rah

tres personas
trehs pehr-soh-nahs

Use para to express, "for a person." For help with using para correctly, see page 236.

I need...

a table | for | three people

Once you feel comfortable Lessons 1-8 , test your mastery of all the concepts with the Mastery Exercises on the CD.

Necesito...

neh-seh-see-toh

el carro
ehl kah-rroh

por
pohr

tres días
trehs dee-ahs

Use **por** to express, "for a time period."
For help with using **por** correctly, see page 235.

I need...

the car   **for**   three days

Make sure you know the Days of the Week (page 191) before moving on to the next Lesson in the Second Week of Spanish!

Spanish Alphabet

a	ah	n	**eh**-neh
b	beh	ñ	**ehn**-yeh
c	seh	o	oh
ch	cheh	p	peh
d	deh	q	koo
e	eh	r	**eh**-reh
f	**eh**-feh	**rr**	**eh**-rreh
g	heh	s	**eh**-seh
h	**ah**-cheh	t	teh
i	ee	u	oo
j	**hoh**-tah	v	veh
k	kah	w	**doh**-bleh veh
l	**eh**-leh	x	**eh**-kees
ll	eh-yeh	y	ee-gree-**eh**-gah
m	**eh**-meh	z	**seh**-tah

The Spanish alphabet contains four letters that are not found in English: **ch**, **ll**, **ñ**, and **rr**.

Spanish Vowels

These are the most important sounds in Spanish
and they will almost always sound the same.

Vowel		Sounds like the...	Spanish Word
a	(ah)	a as in father	casa *(kah-sah)*
e	(eh)	e as in bed, let	mesa *(meh-sah)*
i	(ee)	ee as in meet, feet	libro *(lee-broh)*
o	(oh)	o in old, okay	hotel *(oh-tehl)*
u	(oo)	oo in moon, soon	lunes *(loo-nehs)*

Sometimes two or more letters come together and make another
sound. Don't worry! You'll learn those sounds as they appear!

Sounds of Spanish

c   Before **a**, **o**, **u**, or a **consonant**, like the **k** in *kite*.
Before **e** or **i**, like the **s** in *see*.

cc   Always sounds like the **x** in *tax*.

ch   Like the **ch** in *church*.

d   Usually like the **d** in *dog*. Between vowels or at the end of a syllable, **d** sounds like **th**, as in *that*.

g   Before **a**, **o**, or **u**, hard, like the **g** in *go*.
Before **e** or **i**, soft, like the **h** in *hat*.

h   The Spanish **h** is **always silent!**

j   Like the **h** in *hat*.

Sounds of Spanish

l If only one **l**, it sounds like the **l** in *leave*.

ll The double **ll** sounds like the **y** in *yell*.

ñ Sounds like the **ny** in *canyon*.

r Slightly rolled or trilled.

rr Heavily trilled.

v A cross between **v** and **b**. It is pronounced like a very soft **v**, much like the **v** in *mauve*.

y Like the **y** in *yet* **unless it appears alone,** then it sounds like the **ee** in *feet* and means ***"and".***

z Always sounds like the **s** in *see*.

The letters **k** and **w** are used only to spell words from other languages, such as *kilo, ketchup, Washington.*

Punctuation & Stress

▶ In every Spanish word of more than one syllable, one is always stressed more than the others.

▶ In the infinitive, a verb is stressed on the **last syllable.**
*trabajar (trah-bah-**hahr**)   cantar* (kahn-***tahr***)

▶ In the **present tense** or when used as a **noun**, stress is placed on the **next to last syllable.**
*yo trabajo (yoh trah-**bah**-hoh)* (I work.)
*el trabajo (ehl trah-**bah**-hoh)* (the work)

▶ If a word ends in a **vowel** or the **consonants -s** or **-n**, stress is placed on the **next to last syllable.**
*el sombrero (ehl sohm-**breh**-roh)*
*las manos (lahs **mah**-nohs)*

▶ Direct and indirect question words such as *¿cómo?, ¿cuál?, ¿qué?, ¿dónde?, ¿cuánto?* and others require a written accent.

Punctuation & Stress

▶ Words not following normal stress rules will always have an accent mark indicating which syllable to stress.

*café (kah-**feh**)   avión (ah-**vyohn**)   música (**moo**-see-kah)*

▶ An accent mark is used to distinguish between two words which are spelled the same but have different meanings.

él (he, him)	**el** (the)	**más** (more)	**mas** (but)
tú (you)	**tu** (your)	**dé** (give)	**de** (of, from)
mí (me)	**mi** (my)	**sí** (yes)	**si** (if)

▶ Spanish has an inverted question mark (¿) at the beginning of a question and an inverted exclamation point (¡) at the beginning of an exclamation.

▶ Other rules on accents, stress and syllabification are explained as they occur in each lesson.

Gender

In Spanish, all nouns are classified as being **masculine** or **feminine.** Use the following guidelines to determine gender:

▶ Most nouns ending in **-o**, **-ma** or the consonants **l**, **n**, **r**, **s**, and **all nouns** referring to males are masculine

▶ Most nouns ending in **-a**, **-d**, **-z**, **-ión**, **-dad**, **-tad**, **-tud-**, **ie**, **-umbre**, and **all nouns** referring to females are feminine.

▶ Some nouns keep the same form for both masculine and feminine: *el/la dentista, el/ la estudiante, el/la joven,* etc.

▶ Some nouns are exceptions and must be memorized.
Masculine nouns ending in **-a**: *el mapa, el problema, el clima, el drama, el sofá, el día,* etc.
Feminine nouns ending in **-o**: *la mano, la foto, la moto,* etc.

Plural

Use the following guidelines for making nouns plural:

▶ If the noun ends in a vowel, add an -s:

el libro ➞ *los libros*

▶ If the noun ends in a consonant, add -es:

el hotel ➞ *los hoteles*

▶ If a noun ends in an -s, the noun stays the same but the article changes to its plural form:

el martes ➞ *los martes*

▶ If the noun ends in a -z, the -z changes to a -c and -es is added:

el lápiz ➞ *los lápices*

Numbers 0 - 9

0	**cero**	*seh*-roh
1	**uno**	*oo*-noh
2	**dos**	*dohs*
3	**tres**	*trehs*
4	**cuatro**	*kwah*-troh
5	**cinco**	*seen*-koh
6	**seis**	*says*
7	**siete**	*syeh*-teh
8	**ocho**	*oh*-choh
9	**nueve**	*nweh*-veh

Uno is used only when counting. Before a masculine noun, it becomes *un* and before a feminine noun, it becomes *una.*

185

Numbers 10 - 19

10	**diez**	*dyehs*
11	**once**	***ohn**-seh*
12	**doce**	***doh**-seh*
13	**trece**	***treh**-seh*
14	**catorce**	*kah-**tohr**-seh*
15	**quince**	***keen**-seh*
16	**dieciséis**	*dyehs-ee-**says***
17	**diecisiete**	*dyehs-ee-**syeh**-teh*
18	**dieciocho**	*dyehs-ee-**oh**-choh*
19	**diecinueve**	*dyehs-ee-**nweh**-veh*

Numbers 16 to 29 are usually written as one word: *diecisiete.*
In some countries, they are written as three words: *diez y siete.*

Numbers 20 - 99

20	**veinte**	*vehn*-teh
21	**veintiuno**	*vehn-tee-**oo**-noh*
30	**treinta**	***trehn**-tah*
40	**cuarenta**	*kwah-**rehn**-tah*
50	**cincuenta**	*seen-**kwehn**-tah*
60	**sesenta**	*seh-**sehn**-tah*
70	**setenta**	*seh-**tehn**-tah*
80	**ochenta**	*oh-**chen**-tah*
90	**noventa**	*noh-**vehn**-tah*
99	**noventa y nueve**	*noh-**vehn**-tah ee **nweh**-veh*

To count from 21-99, say the number and add the conjunction *y* (*and*). Example: *treinta y seis* (36).

Numbers 100 - 1,000,000

100	cien	*syehn*
101	ciento uno*	***syehn**-toh **oo**-noh*
200	doscientos**	*dohs **syehn**--tohs*
500	quinientos	*kee-**nyehn**-tohs*
700	setecientos	*seh-teh-**syehn**-tohs*
900	novecientos	*noh-veh-**syehn**-tohs*
1000	mil	*meel*
100,000	cien mil	*syehn meel*
1,000,000	un millón	*oon mee-**yohn***

* *Ciento* (100) is used only in compound numbers like
  ciento uno, ciento dos (101-102), etc.
** Numbers between 200 and 999 agree in gender with the
  nouns they describe: *doscientas personas* (200 people).

Ordinal Numbers

Spanish has ten ordinal numbers. After ten, cardinal numbers are used. They agree in number and gender with the noun.

first	**primero**	*pree-**meh**-roh*
second	**segundo**	*seh-**goon**-doh*
third	**tercero**	*tehr-**seh**-roh*
fourth	**cuarto**	***kwahr**-toh*
fifth	**quinto**	***keen**-toh*
sixth	**sexto**	***sehks**-toh*
seventh	**séptimo**	***sehp**-tee-moh*
eighth	**octavo**	*ohk-**tah**-voh*
ninth	**noveno**	*noh-**veh**-noh*
tenth	**décimo**	***deh**-see-moh*

Ordinal Numbers

Masculine ordinal numbers end in -o and describe el words:
el cuarto piso (the fourth floor).

Exception: When you use *primero* or *tercero* before a **masculine singular word**, the final **-o** is dropped.
el primer día (*the first day*)   *el tercer piso* (*the third floor*)

Feminine ordinal numbers end in **-a** and describe *la* words:
la segunda puerta (*the second door*)

The ordinal number *primero* (*first*) is always used to describe the first day of the month, year, etc.
el primero de enero (*the first of January*)
el primer día del año (*the first day of the year*)

Days Of The Week

Days of the week and months of the year are not capitalized unless they appear at the beginning of a sentence. Notice the Spanish calendar (*el calendario*) begins on Monday.

Monday	el lunes	*ehl **loo**-nehs*
Tuesday	el martes	*ehl **mahr**-tehs*
Wednesday	el miércoles	*ehl **myehr**-koh-lehs*
Thursday	el jueves	*ehl **hweh**-behs*
Friday	el viernes	*ehl **vyehr**-nehs*
Saturday	el sábado	*ehl **sah**-bah-doh*
Sunday	el domingo	*ehl doh-**meen**-goh*

Spanish-speakers never use *en* (*on*), when expressing a certain day. Instead, they use the article *el* or *los*. For example:
  *Salgo **el** lunes. (I'm leaving on Monday).*

Months Of The Year

January	enero	*eh-**neh**-roh*
February	febrero	*feh-**breh**-roh*
March	marzo	***mahr**-soh*
April	abril	*ah-**breel***
May	mayo	***mah**-yoh*
June	junio	***hoo**-nee-oh*
July	julio	***hoo**-lee-oh*
August	agosto	*ah-**gohs**-toh*
September	septiembre	*sehp-**tyehm**-breh*
October	octubre	*ohk-**too**-breh*
November	noviembre	*noh-**vyehm**-breh*
December	diciembre	*dee-**syehm**-breh*

Weather

¿Qué tiempo hace? (**What's the weather like?**)

Weather is generally expressed using the present tense forms of
hacer (*hace*), *estar* (*está*), and *haber* (*hay*). You can also use the
progressive tense (Lesson 20) to discuss an existing condition.

It's sunny.	**Hace sol.**
It's cold.	**Hace frío.**
It's hot.	**Hace calor.**
It's cool.	**Hace fresco.**
The weather's nice.	**Hace buen tiempo.**
The weather's bad.	**Hace mal tiempo.**

Hace (*hacer*) is not used when discussing **rain** or **snow**.
Use *está* (*estar*) and the progressive form of the verb.
Está lloviendo. (*It's raining.*) *Está nevando*. (*It's snowing.*)

Weather

How is the climate?	**¿Cómo es el clima?**
It's clear.	**Está despejado.**
It's cloudy.	**Está nublado.**
It's overcast.	**Está cubierto.**
It's raining.	**Está lloviendo.**
It's snowing.	**Está nevando.**
There is snow.	**Hay nieve.**
There is rain.	**Hay lluvia.**
There are clouds.	**Hay nubes.**
There is a lot of wind.	**Hay mucho viento.**
There are showers.	**Hay lloviznas.**
There is a rainbow.	**Hay un arco iris.**

Family Members

father	**el padre**	*ehl **pah**-dreh*
mother	**la madre**	*lah **mah**-dreh*
son	**el hijo**	*ehl **ee**-hoh*
daughter	**la hija**	*lah **ee**-hah*
brother	**el hermano**	*ehl ehr-**mah**-noh*
sister	**la hermana**	*lah ehr-**mah**-nah*
grandfather	**el abuelo**	*ehl ah-**bweh**-loh*
grandmother	**la abuela**	*lah ah-**bweh**-lah*
grandson	**el nieto**	*ehl **nyeh**-toh*
granddaughter	**la nieta**	*lah **nyeh**-tah*
uncle	**el tío**	*ehl **tee**-oh*
aunt	**la tía**	*lah **tee**-ah*

Family Members

cousin (male)	**el primo**	*ehl **pree**-moh*
cousin (female)	**la prima**	*lah **pree**-mah*
nephew	**el sobrino**	*ehl soh-**bree**-noh*
niece	**la sobrina**	*lah soh-**bree**-nah*
baby	**el bebé**	*ehl beh-**beh***
small boy	**el niño**	*ehl **nee**-nyoh*
small girl	**la niña**	*lah **nee**-nyah*
young boy	**el muchacho**	*ehl moo-**chah**-choh*
young girl	**la muchacha**	*lah moo-**chah**-chah*
husband	**el esposo**	*ehl ehs-**poh**-soh*
husband	**el marido**	*ehl mah-**ree**-doh*
wife	**la esposa**	*lah ehs-**poh**-sah*

Clothing

Clothing	La ropa	*lah roh-pah*
bathing suit	el traje de baño	*ehl trah-heh deh bah-nyoh*
bathrobe	la bata	*lah bah-tah*
belt	el cinturón	*ehl seen-too-rohn*
blouse	la blusa	*lah bloo-sah*
boots	las botas	*lahs boh-tahs*
buckle	la hebilla	*lah eh-bee-yah*
button	el botón	*ehl boh-tohn*
cap (baseball)	la gorra	*lah goh-rrah*
collar	el cuello	*ehl kweh-yoh*
dress	el vestido	*ehl veh-stee-doh*
gloves	los guantes	*lohs gwahn-tehs*

Clothing

jacket	**la chaqueta**	*lah chah-**keh**-tah*
overcoat	**el abrigo**	*ehl ah-**bree**-goh*
pajamas	**las pijamas**	*lahs pee-**yah**-mahs*
panties	**las bragas**	*lahs **brah**-gahs*
pants	**los pantalones**	*lohs pahn-tah-**loh**-nehs*
raincoat	**el impermeable**	*ehl eem-pehr-meh-**ah**-bleh*
sandals	**las sandalias**	*lahs sahn-dah-**lee**-ahs*
scarf	**la bufanda**	*lah boo-**fahn**-dah*
shirt	**la camisa**	*lah kah-**mee**-sah*
shoes	**los zapatos**	*los sah-**pah**-tohs*
shorts	**los pantalones cortos**	*lohs pahn-tah-**loh**-nehs **kohr**-tohs*

Clothing

skirt	**la falda**	*lah **fahl**-dah*
socks	**los calcetines**	*lohs kahl-seh-**tee**-nehs*
sportcoat	**el saco**	*ehl **sah**-koh*
stockings	**las medias**	*lahs **meh**-dyahs*
suit	**el traje**	*ehl **trah**-heh*
sweater	**el suéter**	*ehl **sweh**-tehr*
sweatsuit	**la sudadera**	*lah soo-dah-**deh**-rah*
t-shirt	**la camiseta**	*lah kah-mee-**seh**-tah*
tennis shoes	**los tenis**	*lohs **teh**-nees*
tie	**la corbata**	*lah kohr-**bah**-tah*
underwear	**la ropa interior**	*lah **roh**-pah een-teh-ree-**ohr***
vest	**el chaleco**	*ehl chah-**lek**-koh*

Jewelry

The jewelry	**Las joyas**	*lahs **hoh**-yahs*
bracelet	**la pulsera**	*lah pool-**seh**-rah*
chain	**la cadena**	*lah kah-**deh**-nah*
diamonds	**los diamantes**	*lohs dee-ah-**mahn**-tehs*
earrings	**los aretes**	*lohs ah-**reh**-tehs*
gold	**el oro**	*ehl **oh**-roh*
necklace	**el cuello**	*ehl **kweh**-yoh*
pearls	**las perlas**	*lahs **pehr**-lahs*
ring	**el anillo**	*ehl ah-**nee**-yoh*
silver	**la plata**	*lah **plah**-tah*
watch	**el reloj**	*ehl reh-**loh***

Everyday Necessities

backpack	**la mochila**	*lah moh-**chee**-lah*
batteries	**las pilas**	*lahs **pee**-lahs*
book	**el libro**	*ehl **lee**-broh*
briefcase	**la cartera**	*lah kahr-**teh**-rah*
change	**el cambio**	*ehl **kahm**-byoh*
credit card	**la tarjeta de crédito**	*lah tahr-**heh**-tah deh **kreh**-dee-toh*
film	**los rollos de foto**	*lohs **roh**-yohs deh **foh**-toh*
glasses	**los anteojos**	*lohs ahn-teh-**oh**-hohs*
keys	**las llaves**	*lahs **yah**-vehs*
map	**el mapa**	*ehl **mah**-pah*
magazine	**la revista**	*lah ree-**vee**-stah*

Everyday Necessities

money	**el dinero**	*ehl dee-**neh**-roh*
newspaper	**el periódico**	*ehl peh-ree-**oh**-dee-koh*
passport	**el pasaporte**	*ehl pah-sah-**pohr**-teh*
pen	**la pluma**	*lah **ploo**-mah*
pencil	**el lápiz**	*ehl **lah**-pees*
purse	**la bolsa**	*lah **bohl**-sah*
sunglasses	**los antejos de sol**	*lohs ahn-teh-**oh**-hohs deh sohl*
tickets	**los boletos**	*lohs boh-**leh**-tohs*
umbrella	**el paraguas**	*ehl pah-**rah**-gwahs*
wallet	**la billetera**	*lah bee-yeh-**teh**-rah*
watch	**el reloj**	*ehl reh-**loh***
stamp	**el sello**	*ehl **seh**-yoh*

Colors

Colors	**Los colores**	*lohs koh-loh-rehs*
black	**negro**	*neh-groh*
blue	**azul**	*ah-sool*
brown	**café/pardo**	*kah-feh (pahr-doh)*
gray	**gris**	*grees*
green	**verde**	*vehr-deh*
orange	**anaranjado**	*ah-nah-rahn-hah-doh*
purple	**morado**	*moh-rah-doh*
pink	**rosado**	*roh-sah-doh*
red	**rojo**	*roh-hoh*
white	**blanco**	*blahn-koh*
yellow	**amarillo**	*ah-mah-ree-yoh*

Beverages

I'm thirsty.	**Tengo sed.**	*tehn-goh sehd*
drinks	**las bebidas**	*lahs beh-bee-dahs*
to take a drink	**tomar**	*toh-mahr*
to drink	**beber**	*beh-behr*
beer	**la cerveza**	*lah sehr-veh-sah*
coffee	**el café**	*ehl kah-feh*
decaffeinated	**descafeinado**	*dehs-kah-fey-nah-doh*
diet	**dietética**	*dee-eh-teh-tee-kah*
hot chocolate	**el chocolate**	*ehl choh-koh-lah-teh*
juice	**el jugo**	*ehl hoo-goh*
lemonade	**la limonada**	*lah lee-moh-nah-dah*
milk	**la leche**	*lah leh-cheh*

Beverages

English	Spanish	Pronunciation
punch	**el ponche**	*ehl **pohn**-cheh*
shake	**el batido**	*ehl bah-**tee**-doh*
soft drink	**el refresco**	*ehl reh-**frehs**-koh*
straw	**el popote**	*ehl poh-**poh**-teh*
tea (iced)	**el té (helado)**	*ehl teh (eh-**lah**-doh)*
water	**el agua**	*ehl **ah**-gwah*
wine	**el vino**	*ehl **vee**-noh*
with...	**con...**	*kohn*
without...	**sin...**	*seen*
cream	**la crema**	*lah **kreh**-mah*
ice	**el hielo**	*ehl **yeh**-loh*
sugar	**el azúcar**	*ehl ah-**soo**-kahr*

Desserts

Desserts	**Los postres**	*lohs **poh**-strehs*
cake	**la torta**	*lah **tohr**-tah*
cake (small)	**el pastelito**	*ehl pah-steh-**lee**-toh*
candy	**el dulce**	*ehl **dool**-seh*
cookie	**la galleta**	*lah gah-**yeh**-tah*
custard	**el flan**	*el flahn*
gelatin	**la gelatina**	*la heh-lah-**tee**-nah*
ice cream	**el helado**	*ehl eh-**lah**-doh*
pie	**el pastel**	*ehl pah-**stehl***
pudding	**el pudín**	*ehl poo-**deen***
sherbert	**el sorbete**	*ehl sohr-**beh**-teh*
sweet rolls	**los pasteles**	*lohs pah-**stehl**-ehs*

Fruits

Fruits	**Las frutas**	*lahs **froo**-tahs*
apple	**la manzana**	*lah **mahn**-sah-nah*
apricot	**el albaricoque**	*ehl ahl-bah-ree-**koh**-keh*
banana	**la banana**	*lah bah-**nah**-nah*
cantaloupe	**el melón**	*ehl meh-**lohn***
coconut	**el coco**	*ehl **koh**-koh*
blueberry	**el mirtillo**	*ehl meer-**tee**-yoh*
cherry	**la cereza**	*lah seh-**reh**-sah*
date	**el dátil**	*ehl **dah**-teel*
fig	**el higo**	*ehl **ee**-goh*
grape	**la uva**	*lah **oo**-vah*
grapefruit	**la toronja**	*lah toh-**rohn**-hah*

Fruits

lemon	**el limón**	*ehl lee-**mohn***
mango	**el mango**	*ehl **mahn**-goh*
orange	**la naranja**	*lah nah-**rahn**-hah*
peach	**el melocotón**	*ehl meh-loh-koh-**tohn***
pear	**la pera**	*lah **peh**-rah*
pineapple	**la piña**	*lah **pee**-nyah*
plum	**la ciruela**	*lah seer-oo-**eh**-lah*
raisin	**la pasa**	*lah **pah**-sah*
strawberry	**la fresa**	*lah **freh**-sah*
watermelon	**la sandía**	*lah sahn-**dee**-ah*

A **plátano** (*plah*-*tah*-*noh*) is a cooking banana. It is usually fried or baked and flavored with sugar and cinnamon.

Main Dishes

I'm hungry.	**Tengo hambre.**	*tehn-goh ahm-breh*
chicken	**el pollo**	*ehl **poh**-yoh*
fried chicken	**el pollo frito**	*ehl **poh**-yoh **free**-toh*
pork chop	**una chuleta**	***oo**-nah choo-**leh**-tah*
hamburger	**una hamburguesa**	***oo**-nah ahm-boor-**geh**-sah*
hot dog	**un perro caliente**	*oon **peh**-rroh kah-**lyehn**-teh*
pasta	**la pasta**	*lah **pah**-stah*
rice	**el arroz**	*ehl ah-**rrohs***
with chicken	**con pollo**	*kohn **poh**-yoh*
roast beef	**el rosbif**	*ehl rohs-**beef***
spaghetti	**el espageti**	*ehl ehs-pah-**geh**-tee*
steak	**el bistec**	*ehl **bees**-tehk*

209

Food Preparation & Flavors

Flavor	**El sabor**	Cooked	**Cocido**
bitter	**amargo**	baked	**al horno**
delicious	**delicioso**	burned	**quemado**
dry	**seco**	cold	**frío**
fresh	**fresco**	fried	**frito**
ripe	**maduro**	grilled	**asado**
rotten	**podrido**	mashed	**puré**
sour	**agrio**	raw	**crudo**
salty	**salado**	roasted	**asado**
spicy	**picante**	scrambled	**revueltos**
sweet	**dulce**	tough	**duro**

Furniture

The furniture	**Los muebles**	*lohs **mweh**-blehs*
armchair	**el sillón**	*ehl see-**yohn***
bed	**la cama**	*lah **kah**-mah*
bookcase	**la biblioteca**	*lah bee-blee-oh-**teh**-kah*
carpet	**la alfombra**	*lah ahl-**fohm**-brah*
chair	**la silla**	*lah **see**-yah*
chest (drawers)	**la cómoda**	*lah **koh**-moh-dah*
clock	**el reloj**	*ehl reh-**loh***
curtains	**las cortinas**	*lahs kohr-**tee**-nahs*
draperies	**las colgaduras**	*lahs kohl-gah-**doo**-rahs*
desk	**el escritorio**	*ehl ehs-kree-**toh**-ree-oh*
dresser	**el tocador**	*ehl toh-kah-**dohr***

Furniture

lamp	**la lámpara**	*lah **lahm**-pah-rah*
lampshade	**la pantalla**	*lah **pahn**-tah-yah*
mirror	**el espejo**	*ehl **ehs**-peh-hoh*
plants	**las plantas**	*lahs **plahn**-tahs*
painting	**la pintura**	*lah peen-**too**-rah*
picture	**el cuadro**	*ehl **kwah**-droh*
rug	**la alfombra**	*lah ahl-**fohm**-brah*
sofa	**el sofá**	*ehl soh-**fah***
stereo	**el estéreo**	*ehl ehs-**teh**-reh-oh*
table	**la mesa**	*lah **meh**-sah*
television	**el televisor**	*ehl teh-leh-vee-**sohr***

Set The Table

bowl	**el plato hondo**	*ehl **plah**-toh **ohn**-doh*
candles	**las candelas**	*lahs kahn-**deh**-lahs*
carafe	**la garrafa**	*lah gah-**rrah**-fah*
china	**la loza**	*lah **loh**-sah*
creamer	**la cremera**	*lah kreh-**meh**-rah*
cup	**la taza**	*lah **tah**-sah*
flowers	**las flores**	*lahs **floh**-rehs*
fork	**el tenedor**	*ehl teh-neh-**dohr***
guests	**los invitados**	*lohs een-vee-**tah**-dohs*
glass	**el vaso**	*ehl **vah**-soh*
gravy boat	**la salsera**	*lah sahl-**seh**-rah*
knife	**el cuchillo**	*ehl koo-**chee**-yoh*

Set The Table

napkin	**la servilleta**	*lah sehr-vee-yeh-tah*
pepper shaker	**el pimentero**	*ehl pee-mehn-teh-roh*
plate	**el plato**	*ehl plah-toh*
salad bowl	**la ensaladera**	*lah ehn-sah-lah-deh-rah*
salt shaker	**el salero**	*ehl sah-leh-roh*
saucer	**el platillo**	*ehl plah-tee-yoh*
silverware	**los cubiertos**	*lohs koo-byehr-tohs*
soup bowl	**el sopero**	*ehl soh-peh-roh*
spoon	**la cuchara**	*lah koo-chah-rah*
sugar bowl	**la azucarera**	*lah ah-soo-kah-reh-rah*
tablecloth	**el mantel**	*ehl mahn-tehl*
wine glass	**la copa**	*lah koh-pah*

Trips & Travel

airplane	**el avión**	*ehl ah-**vyohn***
airport	**el aeropuerto**	*ehl ah-eh-roh-**pwehr**-toh*
aisle	**el paseo**	***ehl pah-seh-oh***
arrival	**la llegada**	*lah yeh-**gah**-dah*
baggage	**la contraseña**	*lah kohn-trah-**seh**-nyah*
claim	**de equipaje**	*deh eh-kee-**pah**-heh*
customs	**la aduana**	*lah ah-**dwah**-nah*
departure	**la partida**	*lah pahr-**tee**-dah*
destination	**el destino**	*ehl deh-**stee**-noh*
entrance	**la entrada**	*lah ehn-**trah**-dah*
flight	**el vuelo**	*ehl **vweh**-loh*
gate	**la puerta**	*lah **pwehr**-tah*

Trips & Travel

luggage	el equipaje	*ehl eh-kee-**pah**-heh*
passengers	los pasajeros	*lohs pah-sah-**heh**-rohs*
passport	el pasaporte	*ehl pah-sah-**pohr**-teh*
pilot	el piloto	*ehl pee-**loh**-toh*
porter	el mozo de equipaje	*ehl **moh**-soh deh eh-kee-**pah**-heh*
runway	la pista	*lah **pee**-stah*
seat belt	el cinturón de seguridad	*ehl seen-too-**rohn** deh seh-goo-ree-**dahd***
suitcase	la maleta	*lah mah-**leh**-tah*
ticket counter	el mostrador de boletos	*ehl mohs-trah-**dohr** deh boh-**leh**-tohs*
tickets	los boletos	*lohs boh-**leh**-tohs*

In The Country

In the country	**En el campo**	*ehn ehl **kahm**-poh*
coast	**la costa**	*lah **koh**-stah*
desert	**el desierto**	*ehl deh-**syehr**-toh*
farm	**la finca**	*lah **feen**-kah*
forest	**el bosque**	*ehl **bohs**-keh*
hill	**el cerro**	*ehl **seh**-rroh*
lake	**el lago**	*ehl **lah**-goh*
mountain	**las montañas**	*lahs mohn-**tah**-nyahs*
ranch	**el rancho**	*ehl **rahn**-choh*
river	**el río**	*ehl **ree**-oh*
sea	**el mar**	*ehl mahr*
valley	**el valle**	*el **vah**-yeh*

Travel & Road Signs

caution	**precaución**	*preh-kow-syohn*
closed	**cerrado**	*seh-rah-doh*
curve	**curva**	*koor-vah*
danger	**peligro**	*peh-lee-groh*
detour	**desvío**	*dehs-vee-oh*
emergency	**emergencia**	*eh-mehr-hehn-see-ah*
entrance	**entrada**	*ehn-trah-dah*
exit	**salida**	*sah-lee-dah*
for rent	**se alquila**	*seh ahl-kee-lah*
for sale	**se vende**	*seh vehn-deh*
no entry	**no entrada**	*noh ehn-trah-dah*
one way	**dirección única**	*deh-rehk-syohn oo-nee-kah*

Travel & Road Signs

out of order	**descompuesto**	*dehs-kohm-**pweh**-stoh*
passing lane	**pista para pasar**	***pee**-stah **pah**-rah **pah**-sahr*
push	**empuje**	*ehm-**poo**-heh*
road closed	**camino cerrado**	*kah-**mee**-noh seh-**rah**-doh*
school zone	**zona escolar**	***soh**-nah ehs-koh-**lahr***
slow	**despacio**	*deh-**spah**-see-oh*
stop	**alto**	***ahl**-toh*
stoplight	**el semáforo**	*ehl seh-**mah**-foh-roh*
wait	**espere**	*ehs-**peh**-reh*
walk	**camina**	*kah-**mee**-nah*
wrong way	**via equivocada**	***vee**-ah eh-kee-voh-**kah**-dah*
yield	**ceda el paso**	***seh**-dah ehl **pah**-soh*

Post Office

Post office	**El correo**	*ehl koh-**rreh**-oh*
address	**la dirección**	*lah dee-rehk-**syohn***
addressee	**el destinatario**	*ehl dehs-tee-nah-**tah**-ree-ho*
airmail	**el correo aéreo**	*ehl koh-**rreh**-oh ah-**eh**-reh-oh*
certified	**certificada**	*sehr-tee-fee-**kah**-dah*
envelope	**el sobre**	*ehl **soh**-breh*
insured	**segurada**	*seh-goo-**rah**-dah*
label	**la etiqueta**	*lah eh-tee-**keh**-tah*
letter	**la carta**	*lah **kahr**-tah*
mail	**el correo**	*ehl koh-**rreh**-oh*
mail box	**el buzón**	*ehl boo-**sohn***
money order	**el giro postal**	*ehl **hee**-roh pohs-**tahl***

Post Office

package	**el paquete**	*ehl pah-**keh**-teh*
postage	**el franqueo**	*ehl frahn-**keh**-oh*
postcard	**la tarjeta postal**	*lah tahr-**heh**-tah poh-**stahl***
postmark	**el matasellos**	*ehl mah-tah-**seh**-yohs*
rate	**la tarifa**	*lah tah-**ree**-fah*
scale	**la balanza**	*lah bah-**lahn**-sah*
sender	**el remitente**	*ehl reh-mee-**tehn**-teh*
stamp	**el sello**	*ehl **seh**-yoh*
string	**la cuerda**	*lah **kwehr**-dah*
telegram	**la telegrama**	*lah teh-leh-**grah**-mah*
tape	**la cinta**	*lah **seen**-tah*
zip code	**el código postal**	*ehl **koh**-dee-goh poh-**stahl***

Sports & Equipment

English	Spanish	Pronunciation
ball	**la pelota**	*lah peh-loh-tah*
baseball	**el béisbol**	*ehl bays-bohl*
bat	**la bate**	*lah bah-teh*
basketball	**el básquetbol**	*ehl bahs-keht-bohl*
boxing	**el boxeo**	*ehl bohk-seh-oh*
bowling	**el boliche**	*ehl boh-lee-cheh*
football	**el fútbol americano**	*ehl foot-bohl ah-meh-ree-kah-noh*
golf	**el golf**	*ehl gohlf*
golf clubs	**los palos de golf**	*lohs pah-lohs deh gohlf*
gym	**el gimnasio**	*ehl heem-nah-see-oh*
hockey	**el hockey**	*ehl oh-kee*

Sports & Equipment

horseback riding	**la equitación**	*lah eh-kee-tah-syohn*
mitt	**el guante**	*ehl gwahn-teh*
racket	**la raqueta**	*lah rah-keh-tah*
racquetball	**el ráquetbol**	*ehl rah-keht-bohl*
umpire	**el árbitro**	*ehl ahr-bee-troh*
skating	**el patinaje**	*ehl pah-tee-nah-heh*
skates	**los patines**	*lohs pah-tee-nehs*
soccer	**el fútbol**	*ehl foot-bohl*
swimming	**la natación**	*lah nah-tah-syohn*
team	**el equipo**	*ehl eh-kee-poh*
tennis	**el tenis**	*ehl teh-nees*
volleyball	**el vólibol**	*ehl voh-lee-bohl*

Words To Describe

viejo	old	new	**nuevo**
malo	bad	good	**bueno**
débil	weak	strong	**fuerte**
lento	slow	fast	**rápido**
mojado	wet	dry	**seco**
vacío	empty	full	**lleno**
limpio	clean	dirty	**sucio**
abierto	open	closed	**cerrado**
blando	soft	hard	**duro**
afilado	sharp	dull	**embotado**
estrecho	narrow	wide	**ancho**
el peso	weight	height	**la altura**

Words To Describe

recto	straight	crooked	torcido
profundo	deep	shallow	bajo
apretado	tight	loose	flojo
fácil	easy	difficult	difícil
barato	cheap	expensive	caro
pesado	heavy ⬅🔳➡	light (in weight)	ligero
oscuro	dark	light (in color)	claro
áspero	rough	smooth (surface)	liso
ralo	thin	thick (in density)	grueso
largo	long	short (in length)	corto
frío	cold	hot (to touch)	caliente
blando	mild	hot (to taste)	picante

Words To Describe

viejo	old	young	joven
mayor	older	younger	menor
seguro	confident	shy	tímido
bonito	pretty	ugly	feo
bello	beautiful	handsome	guapo
gordo	fat	thin	flaco
alto	tall ⬅️➡️	short (height)	bajo
nervioso	nervous	relaxed	relajado
normal	normal	strange	extraño
inocente	innocent	guilty	culpable
seguro	sure	uncertain	inseguro
amable	kind	cruel	cruel

Words To Describe

quieto	quiet	loud	alto
loco	crazy	sane	cuerdo
felíz	happy	sad	triste
rico	rich	poor	pobre
barato	cheap	expensive	caro
perezoso	lazy	diligent	diligente
inteligente	smart	dumb	tonto
enfermo	sick	healthy	saludable
valiente	brave	cowardly	cobarde
cortés	polite	rude	rudo
mejor	better	worse	peor
enojado	angry	calm	calmado

Words To Describe

big	big	small	**pequeño**
más grande	bigger	smaller	**más pequeño**
un poco	a little	a lot	**mucho**
más	more	less	**menos**
tan grande	so big	so small	**tan pequeño**
suficiente	enough	too much	**demasiado**
todo	all	none	**ninguno**
ambos	both	several	**varios**
unos	some	none	**ninguno**
el mejor	the best	the worst	**lo peor**

228

Words To Describe

English	Spanish		English	Spanish
ambitious	**ambicioso**		jealous	**celoso**
attractive	**atractivo**		mature	**maduro**
busy	**ocupado**		nice	**simpático**
curious	**curioso**		patient	**paciente**
dangerous	**peligroso**		pleasant	**agradable**
famous	**famoso**		proud	**orgulloso**
fantastic	**fantástico**		romantic	**romántico**
friendly	**amistoso**		ready	**listo**
funny	**chistoso**		scared	**espantado**
honest	**honesto**		surprised	**sorpendido**
impulsive	**impulsivo**		very old	**anciano**
interesting	**interesante**		wise	**sabio**

Portions & Measurements

a dozen	**una docena**	inch	**la pulgada**
a gallon	**un galón**	centimeter	**el centímetro**
a handful	**un puñado**	foot	**el pie**
an ounce	**una onza**	gallon	**el galón**
a pair	**un par**	kilogram	**el kilogramo**
a piece	**un pedazo**	kilometer	**el kilómetro**
a pint	**una pinta**	liter	**el litro**
a pound	**una libra**	meter	**el metro**
a half	**una media**	mile	**la milla**
a quart	**un cuarto**	ounce	**la onza**
a slice	**un pedazo**	pint	**la pinta**
		pound	**la libra**

The Stores

The stores	**Las tiendas**	*lahs **tyehn**-dahs*
bakery	**la panadería**	*lah pah-nah-deh-**ree**-ah*
beauty shop	**la peluquería**	*lah peh-loo-keh-**ree**-ah*
bookstore	**la librería**	*lah lee-breh-**ree**-ah*
candy store	**la confitería**	*lah kohn-fee-teh-**ree**-ah*
clothing store	**el almacén**	*ehl ahl-mah-**sehn***
drycleaner	**la tienda de**	*lah **tyehn**-dah deh*
	lavar en seco	*lah-**bahr** ehn **seh**-koh*
fish store	**la pescadería**	*lah pehs-kah-deh-**ree**-ah*
florist	**la florería**	*lah floh-reh-**ree**-ah*
furniture store	**el almacén**	*ehl ahl-mah-**sehn***
	de muebles	*deh **mweh**-blehs*

The Stores

grocery store	**la tienda de comestibles**	*lah **tyehn**-dah de koh-meh-**stee**-blehs*
jewelry store	**la joyería**	*lah hoh-yeh-**ree**-ah*
laundromat	**la lavandería**	*lah lah-vahn-deh-**ree**-ah*
meat market	**la carnicería**	*lah kahr-nee-seh-**ree**-ah*
newsstand	**el quiosco**	*ehl **kee**-oh-skoh*
pastry shop	**la pastelería**	*lah pah-steh-leh-**ree**-ah*
pharmacy	**la farmacia**	*lah fahr-**mah**-syah*
restaurant	**el restaurante**	*ehl reh-stow-**rahn**-teh*
saloon (beer)	**la cervecería**	*lah sehr-beh-seh-**ree**-ah*
shoe store	**la zapatería**	*lah sah-pah-teh-**ree**-ah*
toy store	**la juguetería**	*lah hoo-geh-teh-**ree**-ah*

Greetings & Courtesies

Hello! Hi! (How's it going?)	¡Hola! (¿Qué tal?)
Good morning!	¡Buenos días!
Good afternoon!	¡Buenas tardes!
What's your name?	¿Cómo se llama?
My name is...	Me llamo...
Nice to meet you.	Encantado.
Same to you.	Igualmente.
How's it going? *(informal)*	¿Cómo te va?
Give my regards to...	Me saluda a...
See you later!	¡Nos vemos!
See you soon! (later)	*¡Hasta pronto! (luego)*
Good night! (Good evening!)	¡Buenas noches!

Survival Phrases

Can you help me?	**¿Puede ayudarme?**
How do you say it?	**¿Cómo se dice?**
How do you spell it?	**¿Cómo se deletra?**
I don't understand.	**No comprendo.**
Do you understand?	**¿Comprende?**
Speak slower.	**Hable más despacio.**
Where is the bathroom?	**¿Dónde está el baño?**
Where are you from?	**¿De dónde eres?**
Excuse me!	**¡Perdón! (¡Disculpe!)**
May I come in?	**¿Puedo entrar?**
I need to find...	**Necesito encontrar...**
Help!	**¡Socorro!**

Por

Use *por* (*for*) to express the following:

Cause, Reason, Motive
Lo hice por ella.
I did it for her.

Means, Method, Manner
Enviado por correo.
Sent by mail.

When Action Takes Place
Salieron por la tarde.
They left in the afternoon.

Frequency
Por una vez cada semana.
Once each week.

Where Action Takes Place
Fueron por las tiendas.
They left for the stores.

Substitution, Equivalence
Él lo cambió por otro.
He exchanged it for another.

Para
Use *para* (*for*) to express the following:

Movement (towards, etc.)
Viene para acá.
He's coming this way.

Use, Purpose
¿Para qué sirve?
What is it for?

Recipient (for someone)
Es para su mamá.
It's for your mother.

Deadline, Time Limit
Lo necesito para mañana.
I need it for tomorrow.

Destination (to a place)
Salieron para Brasil.
They left for Brazil.

Employment
¿Para quien trabaja?
Who do you work for?